When I grow up I want to be a Brownie Leader.

I have lots of different friends at Brownies who don't go to my school.

We are a team!

We care for each other and all of the Brownies are kind.

We all share so it is like a big happy family.

We collected wood and had a campfire with marshmallows. It was very dark when we went home.

Contents

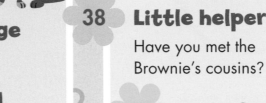

Be safe
You should be able to have a go at everything in your *Brownie Annual*, but sometimes it is a good idea to get some help. When you see this symbol, ask an adult if they can lend a hand.

Web safe
This symbol means you should follow your Brownie Web Safe Code. To remember it, look at page 15 of *Brownie Adventures*.

Badges!
Look out for this sign. If you enjoyed the activity on that page, you might like to try the badge too!

Story time
There's a special story in your *Brownie Annual* – read the beginning on page 8, then pick where you'll go next. Look for this little picture!

WE DISCOVER, WE GROW
Girlguiding

Published by Girlguiding
17–19 Buckingham Palace Road
London SW1W 0PT
info@girlguiding.org.uk
www.girlguiding.org.uk

© Girlguiding 2014
Registered charity number 306016
Incorporated by Royal Charter.

ISBN 978-0-85260-255-3
Girlguiding order code 6005

Printed and bound in the UK by Bell & Bain Ltd

Editor: Jessica Feehan
Writers: Laura Burke, Holly Christie, Rosie Fletcher, Emma Gray-Cornell, Alison Griffiths, Mariano Källfors, Daniel McKeown, Helen Mortimer, Nithya Rae, Alison Shaw, Kat Southgate, Ruth Stone, Emma Thirkill, Helen Thomas
Design Manager: David Jones
Cover Designer: Helen Davis
Designers: Angie Daniel, Helen Davis, Yuan Zhuang
Production Controller: Wendy Reynolds
Photographer: Gemma Huntingford
Brownie Programme Adviser: Helen Channa

Illustrations courtesy of Shutterstock unless otherwise stated. Photography © Girlguiding unless otherwise stated.

Girlguiding would like to thank the following units for their help with this Annual: 1st Bantaskin Brownies, 169th Belfast Brownies, 2nd Brixworth Brownies, 2nd Chalkwell Bay Brownies, 1st East Brixton Brownies, 1st Ecceshall Brownies, 1st Shepperton Brownies, 1st West Dulwich Guides.

Users are reminded that during the lifespan of this publication there may be changes to:
• Girlguiding's policy
• legal requirements
• practice by governing bodies
• British Standards
which will affect the accuracy of the information contained within these pages.

Although the terms 'parent' and 'daughter' are used in this resource, users should remember that what is said may apply to a carer or other adult with parental responsibility, or their ward.

FSC
MIX
Paper from responsible sources
FSC® C007785

What a year!

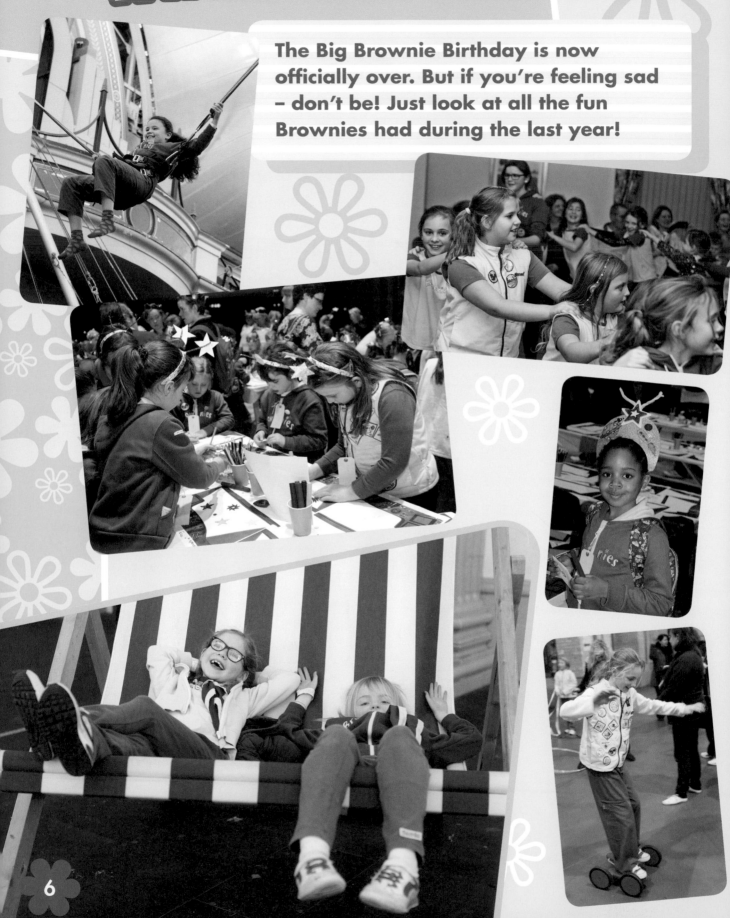

The Big Brownie Birthday is now officially over. But if you're feeling sad – don't be! Just look at all the fun Brownies had during the last year!

What did you do to celebrate Brownies turning 100? Draw a picture or stick a photo here so you'll never forget!

A bubbly treat!

Keep the party going for a little bit longer with a glass of something fizzy for you and your friends – zesty lemonade! Makes five glasses.

1 Cut the lemons in half using a sharp knife. Be safe

2 Using the juicer, squeeze as much juice as you can from the lemons into a jug.

3 Pour an equal amount of cold water into the jug.

4 Stir in the bicarbonate of soda (to make it fizz) and the sugar. You might want to use more or less sugar depending on how sweet you like your lemonade.

5 Add the ice and serve to all your friends.

You will need

- 10 lemons
- Sharp knife
- Juicer
- Jug
- Cold water
- 5tsps bicarbonate of soda
- 5tsps sugar
- Spoon
- Ice
- Glasses (to serve)

Badge link

Hostess

Cook

7

The invisible girl

(part 1)

Once there was a girl called Megan, and she could become invisible.

During school lunch she didn't have to sit with anyone she didn't want to. She found a seat, then vanished. In lessons she never worried about the teacher asking her a tricky question. She kept very still and quiet so he couldn't see her. And at playtime, while the other children spent ages picking a game together, she chose whatever she wanted.

Megan told herself that she was just like the superheroes in the comic books she loved. And that it was pretty cool having a superpower...

Except it wasn't.

One day her mum asked how her day had been and Megan burst into tears.

'Nobody ever sits with me at lunch, Mum. I never get picked for anything by my teacher. And no one asks me to play with them. I'm invisible.'

'Oh, darling, you're not invisible!' her mum replied. 'You just have to speak up and let people know you're there!'

'I try,' sobbed Megan, 'but no one seems to hear me.'

Her mum held her close. 'Your cousin goes to Brownies and she can't stop talking about it. Shall we sign you up? You can try being a whole new, LOUDER Megan there!'

Illustrated by Eglantine Ceulemans

Megan thought about it. Perhaps with new people she really could make a fresh start.

'Let's do it!' she said.

Soon Megan arrived at her first Brownie meeting. Almost immediately two Brownies stopped their game and came up to her. It seemed that at Brownies she was anything but invisible!

'Hi,' said one of the girls. 'I'm Yasmin and this is Ella. What's your name?'

This was her moment! She opened her mouth... And nothing came out.

She tried again. 'I'm Megan.' A teeny tiny whisper. This wouldn't do at all – she needed to say something else or her new identity would disappear.

'What were you playing?' This time she spoke a little louder.

'Tag!' said Ella. 'Do you want to join in?' They'd heard her! It was a small step, but as she ran around the hall with her two new friends, she felt ready to take on the world.

The weeks went by and Megan's voice got bigger and bigger. Then one day she burst through the door and, louder than ever before, called out, 'Brownies, I have something to tell you!'

What is it Megan wants to say? You decide:

❊ *She has read something shocking in the newspaper. (Go to page 37)*

❊ *She has seen something cool happening on the high street. (Go to page 23)*

❊ *She has heard something bad while at the supermarket. (Go to page 11)*

Puzzle time

Pit your wits against these conundrums!
You can check your answers on page 76.

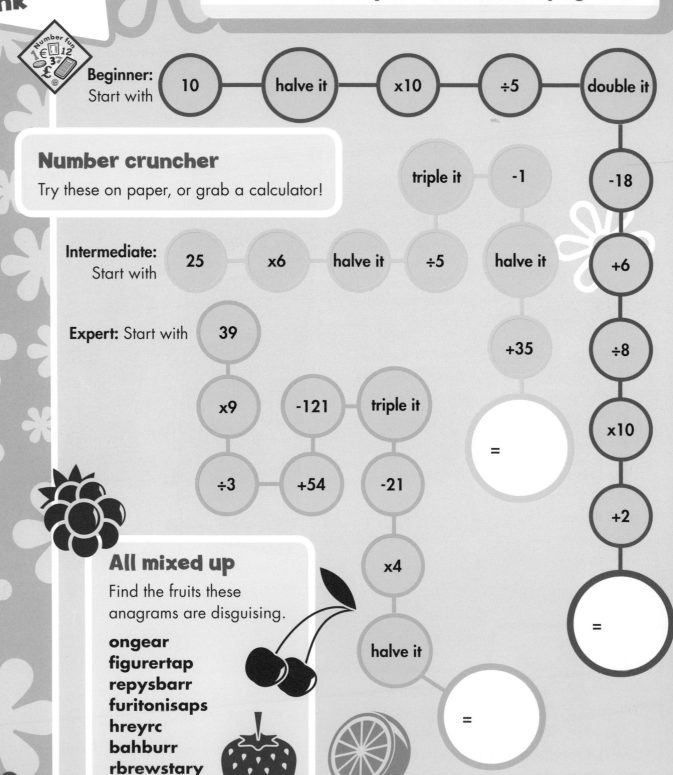

Beginner: Start with — 10 — halve it — x10 — ÷5 — double it

Number cruncher

Try these on paper, or grab a calculator!

triple it — -1

-18

Intermediate: Start with — 25 — x6 — halve it — ÷5 — halve it

+6

Expert: Start with — 39

+35

÷8

x9 — -121 — triple it

=

x10

÷3 — +54 — -21

+2

x4

=

halve it

=

All mixed up

Find the fruits these anagrams are disguising.

ongear
figurertap
repysbarr
furitonisaps
hreyrc
bahburr
rbrewstary

Mind boggler

How many four-letter words can you find in the grid? The letters must be next to each other and in order, but you can move up, down, side to side or diagonally. We've done one (yurt – a type of tent) to get you started!

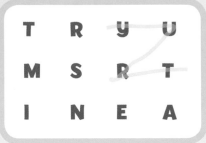

Spot the difference

Can you find ten things that have changed in Picture 2?

Illustrated by Mike Moran

'How did you get that big voice, Megan?!' exclaimed Willow, one of the Brownies' Leaders.

'From coming to Brownies!' laughed Megan. 'Which is why what I want to tell you is so important. My Mum's friend says that her daughter's unit might be closing.'

Willow looked very serious. 'I'm afraid Megan's right, Brownies – there is a local unit that might close. But there are some things we could do to help…'

Who will the Brownies be helping?
❀ *A Brownie unit. (Go to page 72)*

❀ *A Guide unit. (Go to page 51)*

11

Desert island challenge

Imagine you and your friends went to live on a desert island. The sun shines every day, the sea is warm and, best of all, there are no grown-ups telling you what to do!

Let's choose!

What would you want to take with you to your desert island?

If you had to narrow it down to just THREE things, what would they be and why? Write them here:

Now try making some of these tough choices!
1. A dog OR a cow
2. A bicycle OR a canoe
3. A trowel OR some sticky tape
4. A book OR a frisbee
5. A radio OR a phone

What would your friends take?
Find out why!

Trouble in paradise

But who's going to make sure you all have somewhere to sleep and dinner in your tummies? What happens if one of you thinks it's okay to eat the last banana and the others disagree?

You'll need a set of rules to help you all get along and work as a team. But what would your rules be?

1. (Example) Take turns to collect food

2.

3.

4.

5.

6.

7.

8.

9.

10.

'What about a sponsored litter pick?' suggested Megan. 'We can clean up the park and raise money at the same time!'

'What a good idea!' smiled Rowan, one of their Leaders. 'Let's get planning.'

On the big day, the Brownies got to work wearing rubber gloves and their oldest clothes. And before they knew it, there wasn't a piece of rubbish in sight!

'Great job, girls!' cheered their other Leader, Willow. 'And guess how much you've raised… Enough to buy more bins and fix the swings! That'll keep you AND the local wildlife safe.'

Now go to page 70 to find out how the story ends!

Detective Brownie and the Magna Carta mystery

The summer had been long and quiet like a shy snake, and the detective business even quieter, like an even shyer snake. I was itching for a mystery – when in burst my old pal Sophie, clutching a piece of paper.

'DB – I've brought you a mystery!' I leaped to my feet and took the clue from her.

'Kid, looks like you hit the jackpot. I'm gonna teach you how to be a detective!' I looked at the clue, but it didn't make any sense to me or to Sophie.

SGD AQHSHRG KHAQZQX

Change each letter to the next letter in the alphabet to find out where Detective Brownie needs to go!

Scruff, my faithful hound and fellow crime-fighter, barked loudly.

'You've got it Scruff – the British Library! Rule one of being a detective: everyone joins in with solving clues.'

We headed straight for the British Library, my mind racing as fast as my feet – what would we find when we got there? The entrance hall was as a busy as a bee with three jobs. Sophie picked up a leaflet for a special exhibition.

14

Illustrated by Rémy Simard

'But what does it mean?' asked Sophie.

The leaflet Sophie found is in Braille, a special alphabet for blind people – can you work out what it says?

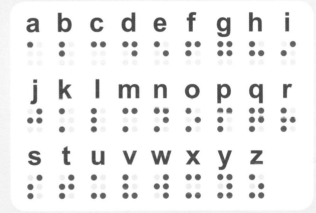

Use this to help you:

'Hmmm… Magna Carta… I think it means Big Cart,' I said, a little unsure. 'Rule two of being a detective: ask good questions. Such as why would they exhibit a big cart in a library?'

Scruff barked loudly. Rushing across different parts of the entrance hall were the museum's director, the head librarian and a security guard. But who had caught Scruff's attention?

Follow Scruff's gaze to decide who Detective Brownie and Sophie should talk to first.

We nodded in agreement and followed the security guard, who looked in a hurry, towards a door marked 'NO ENTRY – SECURITY'.

'Rule three of being a detective,' I said. 'We work as a team.'

We slipped through the security door and up a flight of stairs, following the guard out into a maze of bookshelves.

'We'll never find him!' whispered Sophie, and Scruff barked softly in agreement.

'SHUSH!' came the voice of the librarian we had seen earlier, pointing at a sign.

'NO WHISPERING! NO BARKING SOFTLY!'

Her eyes were darting around, like Scruff with a squirrel. Could she be up to no good? We needed to tell the security guard, and without her seeing us. Sophie scrambled up the nearest bookcase, and we followed her. From here we could see the guard and go along the top of the shelves without being seen.

15

Get across the top of the shelves without being seen!

'Rule four,' I said, climbing off the last bookcase, 'always wear sensible shoes.'

'DB, look!'

The security guard was going through a heavy door, marked 'MAGNA CARTA SECURITY'. Just as we reached the door, it slammed closed in our faces. The door was alarmed and so was I – we had to get the passcode for it.

'It'll be something simple like "1234"' I said, reaching to put in the code.

'Wait! Try "MAGNA CARTA" in numbers,' said Sophie.

The door swung open. 'If we'd done what I said, the alarm would have gone off!' I said. 'Rule five of being a detective: just because I'm in charge, doesn't mean I'm always right.'

We ran through the door to find the security guard scrabbling with the security cameras. He whirled around and turned green at the sight of us.

What's the passcode?

How did you do?

Answers on page 76.

16

'Stop that man!' said a voice behind us. It was the head librarian. 'He's trying to steal the Magna Carta!'

We realised our mistake – the security guard had been in a hurry to steal the Magna Carta, not stop the thief!

Sophie and I rushed forward and grabbed the thieving guard. 'You're coming with us, matey,' said Sophie, hanging on to his arm. Scruff growled through a mouthful of security guard trouser leg.

As the security guard wriggled, I looked around. 'Oh no, he's already got away with it! There's no cart here!' I cried.

'Cart? Detective Brownie, Magna Carta means "Great Charter".' The head librarian reached into the security guard's jacket and pulled out an ancient-looking document. 'King John signed this 800 years ago. It was a set of rules for the King to follow and it gave everyone in the country their rights. It is very important and very valuable – thank goodness it's safe!'

'We've got our own Magna Carta of Being A Good and Fair Detective. Sophie, Scruff, let's add one more.' I took out a lollipop and fixed it in the corner of my mouth. 'When you're dealing with crimes in a library, you always solve them by the book.'

Did you know?

King John's barons made him sign the Magna Carta because they weren't pleased with him – and no wonder! He used to sell their daughters into marriage to raise money for himself. Some of them might have been the same age as you!

Shout out about it

The cone shape of a megaphone helps to make people's voices louder. Try making your own – then you can really shout out about the things you care about!

Badge link

You will need

- Pencil
- Tracing paper
- Piece of A4 thin card or thick paper
- Scissors
- Pictures from magazines
- Craft bits, such as sticky shapes or sequins
- Double-sided sticky tape
- Strip of thin card, about 1.5cm x 12cm

1 Trace the megaphone shape from the next page on to a piece of paper or card. Carefully cut it out.

Be safe

2 Stick on decorations and pictures of the things you want to shout out about. This could be saving endangered animals, celebrating your sporting heroes, looking after your family – whatever you think is important!

3 Turn the shape over and stick a piece of double-sided sticky tape along one of the long straight edges. Peel off the backing tape.

4 Carefully bend the card into a funnel shape. Press the other long straight edge firmly down on to the sticky tape.

5

Make a handle by folding a strip of card into this shape.

6

Stick it to the bottom of your megaphone with double-sided sticky tape.

On the soapbox

Before the days of cardboard boxes and plastic bags, shopping was carried in strong wooden boxes called 'soapboxes'. When people wanted to shout out about anything, they would stand on a soapbox so they could be seen in a crowd. Can you find something to use as a soapbox, so you can really stand up and make your voice heard?

7

Now you are ready to make some noise!

All ears!

Hearing and listening are the same thing, right? Well, not quite! Read on to find out how we hear – and why we need to listen!

You will need

- Large bowl
- Plastic food wrap
- Pinch of uncooked rice
- Baking tray and metal spoon

How do we hear sounds?

Sound travels through the air in waves, which enter your ears and make your ear drums vibrate. The messages from the vibrations travel to your brain, which decodes them.

This experiment lets you 'see' sound waves.

What to do

Stretch the plastic food wrap very tightly over the top of the bowl. Scatter the rice grains on top. Now hold the baking tray close to the bowl and bang it hard with the spoon!

You should see the rice grains jump around, as the sound waves from your bang make the plastic wrap vibrate. This is just how your eardrums work!

Ear, ear!

- Your ears still hear sounds even while you are asleep.

- The smallest bones in the human body are inside the ears.

- Fish do not have ears, but they can 'hear' through ridges on their bodies.

- Some minibeasts hear through tiny hairs on their legs!

Listen up!

It's great to make your voice heard, but what happens if everyone speaks and no one listens? Good listening means concentrating on what you are hearing. Try these ideas to practise being a top listener.

- Play a game of 'Simon Says' with your friends. Listen carefully or you will be out of the game!

- Play your favourite song a few times – listen hard and try to learn all the words.

- Hide a small toy and see if a friend can find it by listening to you tell her which way to go. How well did she listen?

What's your Pow-wow style?

All the most important Brownie decisions are made during Pow-wows. Find out if you're making the most of your chance to have a say!

1. **What's your favourite animal?**
   a) Lion – loud, proud and King of the Jungle!
   b) Dolphin – sociable, clever and likes working together!
   c) Tortoise – loyal, strong and keeps itself to itself.

2. **What three words would you use to describe yourself?**
   a) Loud, enthusiastic, confident.
   b) Friendly, thoughtful, sensible.
   c) Caring, shy, generous.

3. **What would be the best present?**
   a) A karaoke machine!
   b) A day out with your very best friends.
   c) A set of super hi-tech headphones.

5. Where do you see yourself in ten years' time?

a) Surrounded by adoring fans.

b) Having fun with your friends.

c) Living a quiet and peaceful life.

4. You've got the main part in the school play. How do you feel?

a) Over the moon – you can't wait to hear the cheers of the crowd!

b) Really pleased, though you're a little bit nervous too.

c) Shocked – you never auditioned in the first place…

Mostly As

Wow! You always have something to say, and you want to be the first to say it. Having the confidence to make your voice heard is awesome, but make sure you're giving others a chance too.

Mostly Bs

Congratulations – you've got the balance just right. You're great at supporting your Brownie friends by listening to what they have to say, but when you feel strongly about something you will say so.

Mostly Cs

Being a great listener is one of your best skills. Your Brownie friends know that when they speak, you're taking it all in. But they would love to know what you're thinking too – so don't be afraid to speak up!

Her Brownie friends stopped what they were doing and turned to look at her. 'What is it?' asked Yasmin. 'Are you okay, Megan? Has something bad happened?' asked Ella.

'Nothing bad – don't worry!' smiled Megan. 'It's just that at the weekend, while I was out shopping on the high street with my Mum,

I saw a group of people doing something I thought was pretty cool…'

What was the big group of people that Megan saw doing?

❀ *Having a girls-only street party!* (Go to page 67)

❀ *Working together as a community.* (Go to page 53)

A very special place

Have you been to London to see Big Ben? This huge clock and bell are part of the Houses of Parliament, where the laws of the UK are made. And those laws affect all of us!

Power to the people!

The UK is a democracy. This means that the people who live here choose the people who make the laws (Members of Parliament). We do this by voting in an election.

What is an election?

An election is a bit like a Pow-wow at Brownies, where you get to choose something. In an election, people vote by ticking a box on a form. There is an election in 2015 so we might get a new Prime Minister (the person in charge).

Do I get to choose?

Children can't vote, but neither can the Queen so you're not alone! When you are 18 you will be able to vote.

Did you know?

For a very, very long time, women weren't allowed to vote – only men were. Many women thought this wasn't fair, so they fought to be allowed to have their say. These women were called suffragettes and they won their fight in 1918.

Does this matter to me?

Even though you are not allowed to vote, the people in Parliament make a big difference to your life. They make laws to protect you from harm and to make sure you have everything you need to grow into a happy, healthy adult, such as being able to go to the doctor and dentist for free.

'Who looks after the park?' asked Megan. 'Could we talk to them?'

Their Leader Rowan came to the rescue. 'Every area has a local council – a group of people who are responsible for things like parks that everyone shares. You could write to our local councillor.'

So the girls came up with the perfect letter…

…and a month later an envelope appeared, addressed to the Hedgehog Six! Inside was a promise – to make sure that the park would always be a safe place for children (and wildlife!) to enjoy.

Now go to page 70 to find out how the story ends!

Prime Minister you

The Prime Minister is the top dog, the big cheese, the boss. He or she is in charge of how the UK is run. But only because we say so!

Imagine you wanted to be Prime Minister (maybe you do!). Could you come up with an election campaign that would make everyone vote for you? Try this easy guide to winning people's votes!

STEP 1 – Know your audience

Before you begin your campaign, it is important to know what the people who are voting want. Talk to family and friends about what they would like from a Prime Minister.

STEP 2 – Find your focus

You can't please everyone, so choose what you think are the three most important things and make your campaign about those. This is your manifesto. Write it here!

Campaign points:

1.

2.

3.

STEP 3 - Get noticed!

You could make a series of campaign posters, put together a leaflet, design a flag or banner... The more creative your ideas, the better! Fill in the circle with a design for a badge your supporters can wear.

Badge link

Designer

Speaker

STEP 4 - Make a speech

The best way to persuade people you're the right girl for the job is to tell them why! Write a short speech explaining why you should be Prime Minister. If you can, read your speech out to an audience.

STEP 5 - Vote on it

If you made your speech to an audience, have a vote and see whether they'd make you Prime Minister. You could use the homemade ballot box (see below). Or show these pages to someone special and get them to sign on the dotted line if they think you'd be amazing at the job!

Build your own ballot box

Take an old shoebox and carefully cut a slit in the lid, large enough to fit slips of paper through. Use sticky tape to secure the lid to the box and decorate. All you need now is some slips of paper and a pen.

Be safe

You can find more fantastic fun ways of making group decisions on page 28!

Says who?

V.I.D. (very important decisions)

Often the most important decisions aren't up to just you. Write down some things you simply must always decide together as a group (friends and family). How about what film to see next? Or where to go on holiday?

Now comes the fun part. Choose your wacky way of voting and laugh your way to a decision!

Animal talk

Forget voting with your hands... Put some beastly fun into it instead!

Do the woof – go barking for your favourite!

Do the meow – wail away for the purr-fect choice!

Do the binky – jump up and turn around in the air with bunny joy!

Do the bee dance – boogie like a bee to alert others!

Do the stott (or pronk) – jump up in the air on all fours like a gazelle!

Once upon a time

Incredibly unfair voting methods inspired by how things used to be.

The King Says – for hundreds of years, the King decided *everything*. For your group, that means *you*! Awesome! But you may not have friends for long…

The 40-shilling Rule – up until almost 200 years ago, only men earning over 40 shillings a month (about £2,000 today) could decide how to run the country. For your group, only those with at least 40p in their pockets are allowed to help decide.

No Women Allowed – women weren't allowed to help run the country until 1918. This means getting some boys to decide for your group. Boo! Hiss!

Scissors, secrets and cheek

Make voting into a game!

Rock, paper, scissors – play this well-known game as a knock-out competition with winner deciding all!

Secret ballots – write your choice down on paper, fold and put in a bowl. Then count up to find the choice with the most votes!

Sweet talk – hold an open vote, and see who can charm, bribe and beg others to get her way!

Pin the tail – write (or draw) your choices on a large piece of paper, tack it up to the wall, and play pin the tail for a winner!

Super sushi faces

You will need

- Sushi rice (available from lots of supermarkets)
- Vegetables like carrots, seaweed, lettuce, tomatoes, bell peppers and avocado
- Fish and pre-cooked meat such as seafood sticks, smoked salmon, chicken or ham (optional)
- Pea-sized amount of mayonnaise

- Sieve
- Saucepan with lid
- Knife
- Chopping board
- Teaspoon
- A small pastry cutter (any shape)

Badge link

If you've got an hour free at the weekend, why not ask an adult to help you make these fun sushi faces? You can use them to share your feelings with the rest of the world!

1 Put the sushi rice in a sieve and run the cold tap over it to wash it.

2 **Be safe**
Follow the cooking instructions on the sushi rice package – these can vary with different brands. Once you've cooked the rice, leave it to cool.

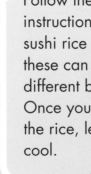

Top tip!

Always wash your hands and tie back your hair before you start cooking. Make sure you wear an apron too!

3 Carefully chop your vegetables, fish and meat into strips or shapes.

4 Ask an adult to help you make sure the rice has cooled all the way through. It should feel sticky. This means you are ready to make your faces!

5 Use the mayonnaise to lightly grease your hands, the pastry cutter and a spoon. Spoon rice into the pastry cutter and squash down firmly with your hands or the spoon. When the pastry cutter is full, ease your sushi face out using the back of the spoon.

6 Make as many sushi faces as you like, then decorate. You can make lots of silly and fun faces, like these!

A day in the life...

You've got a letter! It's from a Brownie friend – but her life and Brownie meetings are a little different from yours...

Hi, I'm Flora.

I'm a Brownie and I live in Blantyre, Malawi. When I'm at home I speak Chichewa, but at school and at Brownies I talk in English.

My Brownie meetings begin after we finish lessons – our Brownie Leader Mary is one of the teachers at my school. But first we take it in turns to help collect water for cooking and drinking. The water pump is 1km from school.

Brownies meet along with Guides and Rangers, so my big sisters Rebecca and Dziwe are also in the meetings. In total, about 60 girls attend each week. I wear a brown dress and a gold scarf that has the colours of the Malawian flag on it.

We do lots of singing and dancing at Brownies. My favourite song is called 'Amavina'. Some evenings, if we are very lucky, we have a campfire at the end of the meeting. And every year we have a camp for all the Brownies, Guides and Rangers. We sleep over at the school and all help to cook, clean and collect water.

I want to be a doctor when I grow up. At Brownies I have learned that I can be anything I want to be if I work hard and always try my best. So I reckon I can do it!

Tell me about yourself!

What would you say in a reply to Flora's letter? She would be very interested in all the things that you do that are different. But she would also like to hear of any ways in which the two of you are the same!

If you're interested in finding out more about Brownies around the world, have a look on **www.wagggs.org**.

web safe

'Did you know that if we lived somewhere else in the world we might not get to go to school?' Megan asked the girls. 'Families with not very much money often just send the boys – they think it's more important for them to be educated!'

The Brownies couldn't believe it – why should boys deserve to read and write and not girls?

Suddenly Rowan, one of their Leaders, interrupted them.

But why?

❀ *To offer to introduce the girls to some amazing women. (Go to page 45)*

❀ *To suggest a crafty way to show boys who's boss. (Go to page 43)*

33

Illustrated by Emma McCann

Follow me!

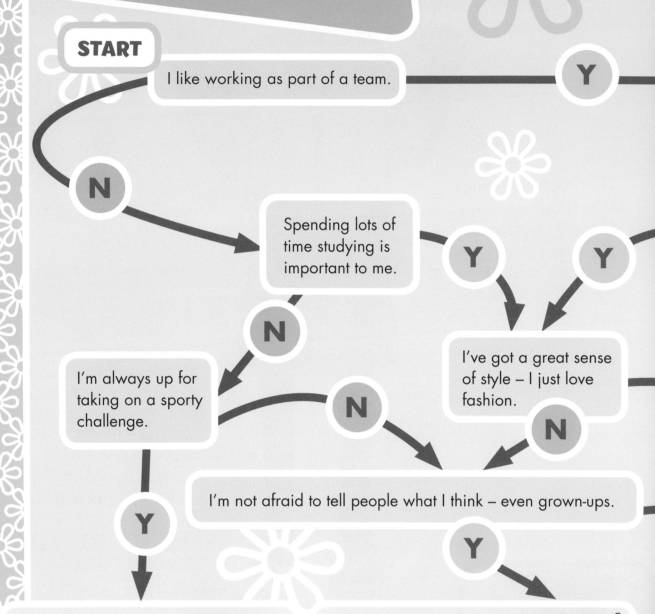

START

I like working as part of a team. — **Y**

N

Spending lots of time studying is important to me. — **Y** **Y**

N

I'm always up for taking on a sporty challenge.

N

I've got a great sense of style – I just love fashion.

N

N

I'm not afraid to tell people what I think – even grown-ups.

Y

Y

Elsa Hammond

© Elsa Hammond

You're a sporty girl with loads of determination, just like Elsa! In June 2014 Elsa challenged herself to row 2,400 miles from California to Hawaii, all on her own. She pushed her mind and body to their limits in the process.

Malala Yousafzai

© ZUMA Press, Inc./Alamy

Studying hard at school is as important to Malala as it is to you. She is originally from Pakistan and has been fighting for girls' right to education since she was 12. She has shown such amazing courage and strength that she was nominated for the 2013 Nobel Peace Prize.

There are some remarkable girls and young women out there, doing wonderful things. And there's nothing stopping you from being one of them! Take this quiz and find out who to turn to for inspiration!

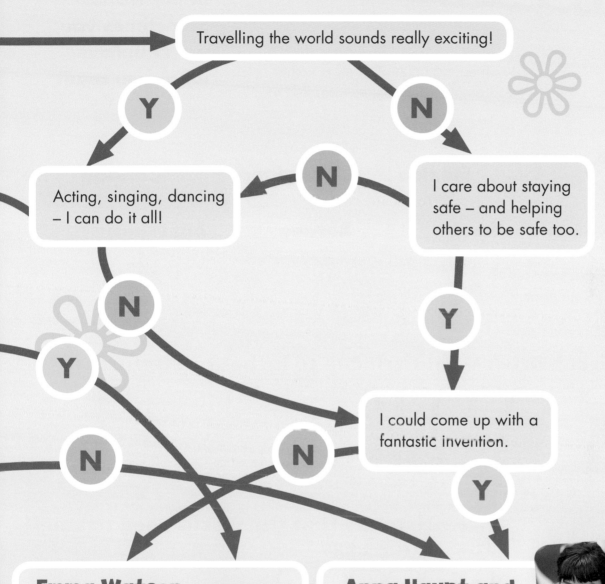

Travelling the world sounds really exciting!

Y

N

N

Acting, singing, dancing – I can do it all!

I care about staying safe – and helping others to be safe too.

N

Y

Y

N

N

I could come up with a fantastic invention.

Y

Emma Watson

With your creative spirit, you're next in line for actor Emma's crown! She's grown up in the spotlight of the Harry Potter film series, but has managed to stay grounded – what a girl!

© epa/Alamy

Anna Haupt and Terese Alstin

Inventive and clever, you have lots in common with Anna and Terese. They designed an invisible helmet to encourage cyclists to be safe on the roads. Their incredible creation won the Venture Cup in 2006.

© Kicki Persson Nordell

Hitting the headlines

Checking out a newspaper is a great way to keep up to date with what's going on in the world. Sometimes you won't believe what you read!

Badge link

Match up the countries below with these amazing headlines from 2014.

Mexico   England   Canada

Spain   Borneo   Australia

1

First British Quidditch cup to be held in Oxford

　　　　　12　　　2　　d

2

Scientists say that the world used to smell like rotten eggs

c　　　　5　　6

3

Thirty baby orangutans saved by a wheelbarrow

　　3　　　1　　e

4

Hundreds of clowns meet for an annual clown convention

☐ ☐ ☐ i ☐ ☐
        8

5

Giant platypus–zilla fossil found

☐ ☐ ☐ t ☐ ☐ ☐ ☐ ☐
  9   10   4

6

Blue-eyed cave men didn't like milk

s ☐ ☐ ☐ ☐
11   7

Now use the numbers to crack the code and reveal the last headline:

☐ ☐ ☐ ☐ ' ☐   ☐ ☐ ☐ ☐ ☐ ☐ ☐ ☐ ☐
12 7 1 4 11   3 1 7 4 4 7 2 5 10

☐ ☐ ☐ ☐ ☐   ☐ ☐ ☐ ☐ ☐ ☐ ☐ ☐
3 1 2 7 5   2 11 10 8 9 5 6 11

w ☐ ☐ ☐ ☐ !
  8 1 4 6

Answers on page 76.

'It must be something pretty important,' joked Yasmin. 'I've never heard Megan speak so loudly!'

'Oh, it definitely is,' said Megan. 'Every Sunday my Dad has a cup of coffee and reads the papers. This weekend there was an article he thought I'd find interesting. He read it out to me while I had my breakfast.'

What was the article Megan's dad wanted to read to her about?

❋ *A girl just like her in another country.* (Go to page 33)

❋ *A cute animal that is becoming extinct.* (Go to page 59)

Little helpers

Brownies, as you know, are named after a magical, helpful and secretive little creature who comes from Scotland. But how much do you know about the Brownie's cousins around the world?

Domovoi

The Domovoi is the Brownie's Russian cousin. Every house supposedly has one. This hairy little fella will protect your home so long as you keep it clean and tidy (and leave him milk and biscuits now and then). He might even predict the future for you! But if you're mean or lazy with housework, he'll start haunting your home like a ghost!

Tomtenisse

This creature is a tiny Scandinavian version of Santa! He even has a white beard and red cap. The Tomtenisse is less than a metre tall, but is incredibly strong. If you're nice to him he'll happily clean your house for you. But if you're rude to him he'll play tricks on you!

Badge link

World cultures

Illustrated by Sandra Aguilar

Kobold

This little house spirit lives in Germany and is smaller than a Rainbow! Usually it doesn't like to be seen and can make itself invisible. If it wants you to see it, it might take the shape of a black cat, a hen, a snake, fire or even a human, so you never know... Keep it fed and it may wash your dishes and sweep your floors for you, and even bring you gifts!

Koro-pok-guru

The koro-pok-guru are 'little people' found in northern Japan. They're small and very agile and they love to fish! They sometimes exchange things with humans, but as they're not keen on being seen, they will secretly leave things for you in the middle of the night.

Trasgu

The Trasgu lives in northern Spain and Portugal. This little creature supposedly walks with a limp, and you can hear him at night when he's up and about. If you're nice to him he'll do your chores for you. Put him in a bad mood, though, and he'll cause all sorts of mischief!

Fizzy fun!

Put some science magic into bathtime by making seriously bubbly bath bombs.

You will need

- Disposable gloves
- 2 cups bicarbonate of soda
- 1 cup cream of tartar
- Mixing bowl
- 1tsp food colouring
- 2tsp food flavouring, eg vanilla, almond, mint
- Spray bottle (with water in)
- Spoon
- Silicone moulds, for example for ice cubes or cookies

1 Put on your gloves and add the cream of tartar and bicarbonate of soda to a bowl. Mix together thoroughly with your hands.

2 Add the food colouring and flavouring, and mix again.

3 Spritz some water into the bowl and keep mixing. Add just a little water at a time until the mixture is still crumbly, but will just about hold together if you squeeze it tightly in your hand.

Badge link

Illustrated by Jackie Stafford

4

Using a spoon, scoop the mixture into your silicone moulds and press down firmly.

5

Leave to dry somewhere warm overnight. The next day, turn the moulds over and tap them gently to ease the set bombs out.

Top tip!

Wrap your bath bombs in cellophane or tissue paper tied with a ribbon and give them as gifts. Or sell them to raise money for a good cause – then you could ask your Leader about getting this great new badge!

How does it work?

Bath bombs are made from ingredients that are unreactive when dry, but when they get wet they effervesce (fizz) and eventually dissolve. The bubbles are made from carbon dioxide.

Bee part of a good cause

Bees help us grow food by pollinating plants, and we use their yummy honey in loads of things, from food to soap. But the UK's bees are disappearing – we can't let that happen!

How can I help?

- Plant bee-friendly flowers in your garden or window box, school or meeting place.
- Make sure there is water in your garden, for example in a bird bath.
- Try to leave somewhere for bees to nest, like a pile of dry plant stems or logs.
- Buy local, British honey and honey products.
- Make this cute felt bee brooch!

You will need

- Scissors
- Templates (provided on opposite page)
- Felt (yellow, white and black, approximately 4cm x 7cm)
- Black felt-tip pen
- 25mm brooch back fastener/safety pins
- PVA glue

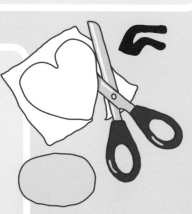

1 Use the templates to cut out all the parts for your bee from felt – one yellow bee body shape, one white wing shape and one black antennae shape.

2 Glue the wings and antennae to the back of the bee's body. Leave to dry completely.

42

Illustrated by Molly Sage

3 Using the black felt-tip pen, draw on two eyes and a mouth for your bee and some black stripes on the bee's tummy.

4 Finally, glue a brooch back fastener or a safety pin on to the back of your bee. Leave to dry completely.

5 Now wear your bee brooch to show you care!

Craft

Friend to animals

Wildlife explorer

Environment

I ♥ BEES

Rowan pointed to Megan's sash. 'Your Six badge lets everyone know you're part of a special group. Lots of badges do this. I have a daffodil badge that shows I support a cancer charity, for example.'

Megan thought carefully... 'So we could make badges to tell people girls are as special as boys!'

'Let's start with stickers,' laughed Rowan. 'I have some blank ones here.'

At the end of Brownies, Megan wore her favourite sticker home. It said: 'Girls and boys look different. Our brains are the same!'

Now go to page 70 to find out how the story ends!

Fairtrade tea party

Look out for the Fairtrade mark.

FAIRTRADE

Fair trade means that farmers and workers around the world are paid fair prices and can work in better conditions. Now that's something worth celebrating!

Tea party checklist

☐ Choose a venue. Are you going to hold your tea party at your house? At Brownies? Or even at school? Make sure you ask an adult for permission before making firm plans.

☐ Pick a time and date. Again, check with the adults involved whether it's possible.

☐ Get the food. Take a trip to your local shop or market and find as many Fairtrade products as you can for your party – then write your menu. For Fairtrade recipes, visit **www.fairtrade.org.uk/recipes**.

Web safe

☐ Design and send out the invitations. You'll need to include all the information so people know where and when to come.

☐ Don't forget drinks! You can also buy Fairtrade tea, herbal tea, coffee and fruit juices. Make a list of the products you find so that you can tell people about them and where they can buy them in your local area.

Badge link

Hostess

Cook

Get ready for the party. If you're running the event as a group, share out the tasks – there'll be lots to do! You'll need to prepare the food, pour the drinks and set up the venue (lay out chairs, tables, decorate).

Enjoy yourself! Don't forget to tell people about the Fairtrade products you've used and talk to them about how fair trade works. Encourage them to get involved too!

Try it this way

Even if you can't actually hold a tea party, planning is half the fun and a useful skill to have. And for a make-believe party you can spend as much as you like!

'Since I know loads of women who think girls deserve all the same stuff as boys,' said Rowan, 'shall we invite them to a special end-of-term party…?'

And what a success the party was!

'I talked to a real artist about my paintings!' beamed Yasmin.

'I met a doctor who fixes people's brains!' squealed Lily.

They all agreed that was pretty cool. Megan's favourite, though, was the lady who went to other countries and set up libraries so girls would have books to read – how amazing is that?

Now go to page 70 to find out how the story ends!

Tree teasers

Step into the woods with these fun puzzles all about trees. Don't forget to check your answers on page 77 when you've finished!

Forest maze

Find the path through the forest, answering the questions as you go.

1. Which tree's seeds are called 'keys'? Oak   Ash

2. What is the world's tallest tree? Scots pine   Coast redwood

3. Which sweet treat comes from tree sap? Honey   Maple syrup

4. Which animal lives in eucalyptus trees? Koala   Bush baby

You're through the woods!

Badge link

Wildlife explorer

Illustrated by Mike Moran

Love your leaves

Which trees do these leaves come from?

Oak Beech Rowan
Maple Holly Willow

1.

2.

3.

4.

5.

6.

Fruity fun

Find these fruit tree names in the grid. But be warned – one of these fruits doesn't grow on a tree and isn't in there. Which one?

Apple   Mango
Apricot   Orange
Cherry   Peach
Damson   Pear
Lemon   Pineapple
Lime   Plum

M	T	N	D	B	N	O	M	E	L
C	A	O	E	A	H	S	G	P	I
A	P	R	I	C	O	T	O	E	M
H	P	A	P	H	I	M	L	A	E
N	L	N	K	E	A	B	N	R	I
O	E	G	O	R	F	G	E	S	C
S	C	E	M	R	O	F	R	M	E
M	A	R	I	Y	E	C	P	U	A
A	L	B	N	A	W	J	D	L	H
D	E	C	P	H	C	A	E	P	M

J 'oak' corner

What do elephants and trees have in common?
They both have trunks!

What kind of tree can you fit into your hand?
A palm tree!

What did the little tree say to the big tree?
Leaf me alone!

How do trees get on to the internet?
They log in!

47

Say it with scraps

You will need

- Scissors
- A full-length photo of yourself
- A4 card
- Glue stick
- Old newspapers and magazines
- Coloured card
- Pen
- Coloured pencils
- Glitter, glitter glue, sequins, stickers (optional)

Keeping a scrapbook is a great way of collecting your thoughts, feelings and memories and showing people what's important to you. Design your first scrapbook page on the theme 'Why I love being me...'.

Badge link

1

Cut around the photo of yourself, making sure to remove all of the background.

2

Glue the photo in the middle of the piece of card.

3

Using the old newspapers and magazines, cut out the individual letters to make up your name and stick these on the card wherever you like. You could keep them close together so they're easy to read, or space them out.

Illustrated by Molly Sage

4

Now cut out some speech bubble shapes from coloured card and write on the names of the people who are important to you. Stick these on the card around your photo.

5

Go through the newspapers and magazines to find pictures that show the things you love, then cut them out. If you're into science then you might use a picture of a microscope. Or if you love your pet, cut out a cute kitten.

6

Stick your pictures in between the speech bubbles. If you've got any space left, decorate it using the coloured pencils and any stickers, glitter or sequins you have available.

Top tip!

You can make your scrapbook page about absolutely anything! So why not use the same instructions but for a different theme. Here are some ideas:
- Being a Brownie...
- If I could change the world...
- When I grow up...

It's great to be a Guide!

Who better to give you the inside scoop on what it's like to be a Guide than Guides themselves? These girls have got some important things to tell you! They might even be from a unit near you...

Why did you become a Guide?

'Brownies was fun and I wanted to see if Guides was just as fun – and it was!'
Jaydean, 12

'I really wanted to come to a club where I could just have fun with no worries.'
Olivia, 11

'For the different opportunities and life skills I would learn.'
Hannah, 11

'To stay in contact with old friends and to make new ones.'
Lola, 12

'My Mum went when she was younger and I wanted to get more badges than her!'
Mya, 12

'When I was at Brownies I often saw the Guides laughing and having fun. I also wanted to feel more independent.'
Amelie, 11

What's the best thing about being a Guide?

'I really enjoy the stuff that the Leaders prepare for us. If you want to go to Guides, I recommend you come to my unit – you will really enjoy it!'
Anniece, 12

'The thing I enjoy most is meeting new people outside of school and having fun!'
Pollyanna, 10

'My favourite part of Guides is Patrol time because I get to talk to people I wouldn't talk to as much.'
Olivia, 13

'I love it when we have fun! Cooking, crafts, games and, most of all, camps.'
Eve, 12

'I've most enjoyed going on camp and the opportunity to do volunteering.'
Juliet, 14

'The best thing about Guides is my Leader, duh! She is the role model of the year.'
Sarah, 10

Willow explained that their local Guide unit had just one Leader, who was finding it tough on her own.

'What if we told people all the reasons we want to be Guides?' suggested Megan. 'Maybe someone would want to help!'

The Brownies thought this was a great idea, and together they made a huge poster to put up.

Some weeks later, Willow arrived at Brownies smiling – a lady had seen the poster and called to ask about helping at Guides. 'Great work, Brownies,' said Willow.

Now go to page 70 to find out how the story ends!

What's the password?

Badge link

Computer

For lots of online games you need a password – this locks up your information so that only you can access it. A password you've put serious thought into will keep you super-safe online.

Golden rules

1. **It has to be hard to guess:** Your pet's name won't do! You don't need to be Detective Brownie to guess that easily!

2. **It has to be memorable:** Forgetting your password is like losing your door key. It's very annoying and you look a bit silly!

3. **It has to be different:** Obsessed with Moshi Monsters AND Club Penguin? Make sure you don't use the same password for both. And remember to change passwords regularly.

1. Lock it down

Create your password using a combination of letters and numbers. It should be at least six characters long. If you want to make it really strong, include both upper- and lower-case letters, numbers and a special character like @ or #. And remember not to use repetition or sequences such as aaa1234.

2. Check it

Ask some of your friends and family to try to guess what your password might be. Anyone get it? No? Well done you!

WARNING

Crack the code

Use the first letter of each picture to find the secret password.

 _____

 _____

 _____

 _____

 _____

Check your answer on page 77.

Automatic fail!

Did you write your password down? That means anyone can read it. Oops! *Never reveal your password to anyone* (your parents or a trusted adult are ok)!

Brownie Web Safe Code

Putting your password to good use online? Always remember your Brownie Web Safe Code. Check it out on page 15 of your *Brownie Adventures* book or on the Brownie website: **www.girlguiding.org.uk/ brownies**.

Web safe

'So, they were picking up litter…' began Megan.

'Ewwwww! With their hands?!' squealed Fatima. 'That's not cool!'

Megan snorted. 'Ok, firstly, they were using those grabber things. And secondly, it was cool – everyone was working together to make the place nicer.'

'Maybe they could do something about our park,' suggested Yasmin. 'It's always full of rubbish and the swings are broken.'

'Why don't WE do something about it?' exclaimed Ella.

What do the girls decide to do?
* *Get their hands dirty on a unit outing. (Go to page 13)*

* *Go straight to the top! (Go to page 25)*

Quiz-tastic!

Get some friends together and challenge them to take part. You can be Quiz Master and ask the questions, or take turns with your friends so you can try guessing too!

Who am I?

Read clue (a) about a famous person – real or from books, films or TV. If you guess correctly who it is, you get 5 points. Otherwise, read clue (b). If you get the correct answer now, you score 3 points. You have one final clue (c) to guess, and if you do, you get 1 point.

1

(a) I have two sisters, called Lisa and Maggie.

(b) I sometimes say things like 'Eat my shorts' and '¡Ay, caramba!'.

(c) I'm in a TV show and I wear a red T-shirt and blue shorts.

2

(a) My best friends include a boy, a pig, a tiger, an owl, a kangaroo and a donkey.

(b) I love honey and spend lots of time searching for it.

(c) I am a bear and I live with my friends in Hundred Acre Wood.

3

(a) I was born in Germany and did a lot of work in an area of science called 'relativity'.

(b) I wrote what is sometimes called the 'world's most famous equation' ($e = mc^2$).

(c) If you are very clever, your friends might call you by my name.

4

(a) I was the daughter of Henry VIII and Anne Boleyn.

(b) People sometimes called me 'Good Queen Bess'.

(c) I was Queen of England for 44 years and the current Queen has the same name as me.

5

(a) I was a prisoner for 27 years and was given the Nobel Peace Prize in 1993.

(b) I died in December 2013 at the age of 95.

(c) I was the first black president of South Africa.

Picture it

1 Which country is this a map of?

2 2. Who is this?

© ALLSTAR Photo Library/Alamy

3 What scientific event does this show?

4 Name this famous painting – and for a bonus point name the painter.

5 What is this a close up of?

What's the link?

Each set of words has something in common, but what is it?

1. Bagels, chapattis and pitta?
2. Ulna, radius and humerus?
3. Sahara, Thar and Gobi?
4. Maris Piper, King Edward and Charlotte?
5. Rose, thistle, shamrock and leek?

Literary legends

Match the book or film with the heroine.

Katniss Everdeen

Andrea (Andy)

Belle

Dorothy

Hermione Granger

The Wizard of Oz

The Hunger Games

Harry Potter and the Philosopher's Stone

Beauty and the Beast

The Suitcase Kid

Answers on page 77.

Edible engineering

This activity is supported by

 Rolls-Royce

to inspire our future scientists and engineers.

You will need

- Stack of books
- Five thin rectangular chocolate bars
- Plastic cup
- Coins or weights
- Plastic bottle
- Hot water
- Fridge

In *Charlie and the Chocolate Factory*, Willy Wonka builds a whole palace out of chocolate for an Indian prince. Can you build a chocolate bridge?

1 Pile the books into two equal-sized stacks with a small gap between them. This is the ravine your bridge will go across!

2 Lay one chocolate bar across the gap. Place the plastic cup on top.

3 Start adding coins or weights, a few at a time, until it breaks. Make a note of how much weight it could hold.

Badge link

56

4

Now carefully fill a plastic bottle with hot (but not boiling) water. Press the long edge of one chocolate bar against it for a few seconds, until it starts to melt.

Be safe

5

Stick the melted edge to the long edge of another bar and leave in the fridge to set. You might need to prop it against the side so that it stays in shape.

6

Repeat so you have two L-shaped pieces.

7

Once they have set, stick the two pieces together into a long box shape, and leave to set again.

8

Test out your bridge in the same way. How much weight can it hold this time before breaking? If you've stuck it together correctly, the box shape should make your bridge stiffer and stronger!

Take it further

Web safe

If you liked this experiment, why not check out some more fun ideas from Rolls-Royce? Go to **www.girlguiding.org.uk/ brownies** > Badges to find out more.

Where's my baby?

Untangle the maze to help each animal find its baby. And be quick – all of these cute creatures are endangered, so there aren't many of them left!

Giant Panda

Leatherback Turtle

Goliath Frog

Barn Owl

African Penguin

Giant Armadillo

Blue Whale

Sometimes I eat plastic bags by mistake, because they look like jellyfish in the water

I can grow up to 33cm long – the size of a dinner plate!

I'm also called White Owl, Cave Owl, Monkey-faced Owl, Hissing Owl or Delicate Owl

I have huge claws on my front feet and up to 100 teeth

I lay my eggs in a hole dug in guano (old droppings) – yuk!

I have five fingers AND a thumb to help me eat bamboo

Owlet

When my baby is born it weighs as much as an adult hippo!

Calf

Tadpole

Cub

Chick

Pup

Hatchling

Badge link

Did you know?
Animals can become endangered because the places they live in are destroyed, or they can't find enough food, or they're eaten by humans.

Why not join the World Wildlife Fund's Go Wild Club (**www.wwf.org. uk/gowild**) and explore your wild side while helping endangered animals!

Web safe

'The article was about hedgehogs – our Six animal,' explained Megan. 'There aren't as many as there used to be.'

'But why?' gasped Lily.

'Well, one problem is litter. They can get stuck in it, or even eat it! Our park must be so dangerous for hedgehogs. It's horrible enough for humans, with all that rubbish and the broken swings.'

'Why don't you do something about it, girls?' suggested Rowan, one of their Leaders.

But what do the girls do?
* *Become hedgehog environmentalists! (Go to page 13)*

* *Write a letter to make a big difference. (Go to page 25)*

Prickly party food

You will need

- 225g butter
- 175g caster sugar
- 1 egg
- $\frac{1}{2}$ tsp vanilla extract
- 300g plain flour
- 1 tsp baking powder
- $\frac{1}{4}$ tsp salt
- 100g milk chocolate
- 50g crushed walnuts, desiccated coconut, sprinkles or vermicelli

- Wooden spoon
- Mixing bowl
- Sieve
- Toothpick or skewer
- Baking tray lined with a sheet of baking paper
- Oven gloves
- Heatproof bowl
- Saucepan
- Metal spoon

Bake these cute cookies and share them with your friends!

1 Preheat the oven to 190°C/gas mark 5.

2 Use the wooden spoon to beat the butter and sugar together in a bowl. Then add the egg and vanilla extract.

3 Sieve in the flour, baking powder and salt, and mix until the mixture looks like crumbs.

4 Now squash a handful of crumbs together and roll between your hands until you make a lump the size of a golf ball.

Illustrated by Molly Sage

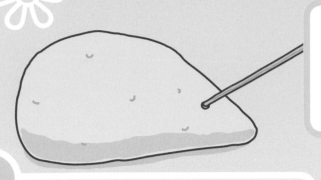

Top tip!

Always wash your hands and tie back your hair before you start cooking. Make sure you wear an apron too!

5

Gently mould the ball into a pear shape to make the hedgehog's body. Use the toothpick to make marks for eyes.

6

Place each hedgehog cookie on the baking tray and bake for 6 to 8 minutes.

Be safe

7

Carefully remove the cookies from the oven using oven gloves. Leave to cool while you melt your chocolate – break it up and put in a bowl over a pan of hot water, then heat gently.

Be safe

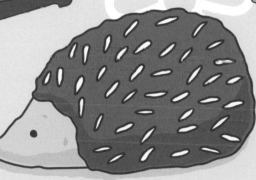

Badge link

8

Spoon chocolate over the round end of each hedgehog and sprinkle with your chosen 'spikes'. Then leave to set.

9

Enjoy!

Did you know?

Real hedgehogs don't like heat, so remember to check bonfires before you light them in case they are hiding inside!

Number safari

Odd number out

Solve the animal clues using the numbers below –
but be careful, one of them doesn't fit!

a. How many legs would you expect to find on a centipede?

b. How many Dalmatians are there in the name of the book (and film)?

c. If an ostrich lays a dozen eggs, how many does she have?

d. Each section in a bee's honeycomb is a hexagon. How many sides does this shape have?

e. Six sick sheep sip strawberry slushies. What a tongue-twister! But how many legs are there on six sheep?

f. We all know that spiders have eight legs. Do you know how many eyes they have?

Numbers: 6, 24, 100, 8, 4, 101, 12

Animal name creator

Come up with an animal that's unique to you.

How many letters in your first name?
2: Cuddly
3: Giant
4: Blue
5: Speedy
6: Miniature
7: Lesser-spotted
8: Long-tailed
9 or more: Feathery

Badge link

Illustrated by Mike Moran

Leap to safety

Answers on page 77.

This little frog is trying to find her way across the pond.
Where should she start to avoid the snakes and reach the other side?

- The red lily pads make her jump forward two spaces.
- Green ones make her move back one.
- Yellow ones make her jump forward three spaces.
- Blue ones make her jump back two spaces.

START 1   START 2   START 3

HOME

How many letters in the name of the month you were born?

3: Burrowing
4: Jumping
5: Diving
6: Climbing
7: Singing
8: Running
9: Gliding

What happens when you multiply the first two numbers together?

6–20: Mouse
21–30: Parrot
31–40: Frog
41–50: Shark
51–60: Beetle
61–70: Dolphin
71 or above: Gazelle

**Example: Jessica, born in April –
Lesser-spotted Diving Frog (7, 5, 35)**

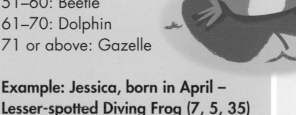

Can you draw your creature? What special features (like wings or a tail) would it need?

Reflect yourself

Draw a picture of yourself in the 'mirror' below. You could be wearing your favourite clothes! Then write words in the boxes to show what you're like on the inside. You might add 'musical' if you like singing, or 'kind' if you like looking after animals.

Now ask a friend to draw you as well. What did she notice that you didn't? Do you think your picture or her picture was more accurate?

People come in all shapes and sizes – what don't people see when they look at you?

64

Illustrated by Emma McCann

Do you know the phrase 'don't judge a book by its cover'? Here are some other great quotes!

There are no bad pictures; that's just how your face looks sometimes – Abraham Lincoln

Let your smile change the world; don't let the world change your smile – Anonymous

Love looks not with the eyes, but with the mind – William Shakespeare

If you have good thoughts they will shine out of your face like sunbeams and you will always look lovely – Roald Dahl

Do you know any more sayings like this? Can you make one up?

I'm a girl and I can...

In the past girls were told they couldn't run about, be astronauts, vote or even own a house. It's easy to be put off when something's difficult or people say it's not for you, but this paper chain will help you remember that you can do anything!

You will need

- Strips of coloured paper around 20cm x 2cm
- Pens or pencils
- Glue stick

1
Think of something you are good at, like drawing or running. Write it on a strip of paper and stick the ends together to make a loop.

2
Now think of something you used to find really hard but can now do more easily. Maybe you're a lot better at riding your bike, or spelling! Write it on another strip of paper and link it to your first loop.

3
Keep thinking of more things, and loop each one through to make the chain longer. Whenever you complete a new challenge you can add that too.

4
Stick your chain up somewhere you can see it to remind you that you are always learning.

Wear it!

We all know that girls are amazing, and that they can do anything they want to do! And now you can tell other people how great girls are with this brilliant new 'Girls can' wristband, badge and notecards.

You can see all the great 'Girls can' items  at **www.girlguidingshop.co.uk**. Just remember, when anyone asks you about them, tell them how great it is to be a girl – and a Brownie!

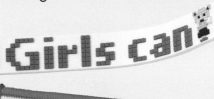

'I saw the same thing!' piped up Louise. 'Loads of women dancing and laughing.'

'I was there!' interrupted Rowan, one of their Leaders. 'It was International Women's Day. A day to celebrate how amazing we are and make sure we are treated equally.'

'Why didn't you invite us?' asked Megan.

'We're women too – or we will be one day!'

Rowan grinned. 'Maybe there's a way I can make it up to you…'

What is Rowan's idea?

❀ *They have their own party at Brownies!*
(Go to page 45)

❀ *A cool activity to do RIGHT NOW.*
(Go to page 43)

What's inside?

It's what's inside that really counts! Surprise your friends with these beautiful (and edible) dyed eggs!

You will need

- Egg
- Water
- Food in bright colours – chopped red cabbage (purple), onion skins (brown) and spinach (green) all work well
- 2tbsp white vinegar

- Saucepan
- Timer
- Slotted spoon
- Egg box
- Sieve
- Jug
- Fridge

1

First, boil your egg. Place it in a saucepan with enough cold water to cover it and heat until the water boils. After ten minutes, remove the egg using the slotted spoon and run it under cold water for a minute. Leave to cool in the egg box.

Be safe

2

While your egg's cooling, make your first dye! In the saucepan, heat two handfuls of your chosen food and 250ml water. Let it bubble for 15 minutes, and then allow it to cool.

Be safe

68

Illustrated by Jackie Stafford

3 Carefully pour the dye through a sieve into a jug, then add two tablespoons of vinegar. Lower your egg into the dye and leave in the fridge for several hours (or even overnight).

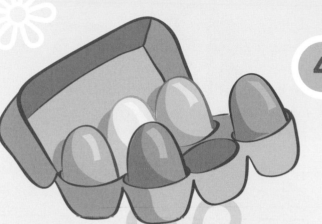

4 Once you like the colour, lift the egg out and leave to dry in the egg box. Try other foods to see the different colours you can make! Be aware that your natural food colouring won't be as bright as some of the treats you see in the shops – but it's better for your body.

5 If you want to eat your egg, just keep it in the fridge and get munching within a couple of days.

Try it this way!

You could wrap elastic bands around the eggs before dying to create cool stripy patterns.

69

The invisible girl
(part 2)

As she climbed on to the bus home, Megan had so much to say that the words tumbled out of her mouth in a muddle.

'Slow down!' exclaimed her dad. 'I can tell you're excited, but I have no idea what you just said!'

Megan took a deep breath and began again. She told her dad all about her big moment at Brownies – how everyone had listened to her, and how because of her the whole unit had made something wonderful happen.

'Have you heard this?' Megan's dad called as he dropped her off at the front door. 'Our Megan's found her voice!'

'Sounds like Brownies did exactly what we hoped it would do then!' said her mum.

Megan nodded. Now if only she could be the new version of herself at school too…

***

The next day Megan woke up with a strange feeling in her tummy.

She thought about it carefully as she munched her breakfast. Usually before school it felt like her stomach was full of worms – all wriggly, like she might be sick. But this felt more like excited butterflies. Maybe today was going to be a good day!

Illustrated by Eglantine Ceulemans

The excited feeling lasted all the way to school, and as she lined up in the playground the tickly butterflies made her smile to herself.

Aisha, the girl next to her, smiled back.

Megan was stunned. Normally the other kids looked right through her. She looked around – maybe Aisha was really smiling at someone behind her. But there was no one there.

By lunchtime the butterflies had faded but Megan was feeling better than ever. She had managed a whispered offer to share colouring pencils with the boy who sat next to her, and had even put her hand up to answer a tricky maths question – much to her teacher's surprise.

And as she crossed the playground there was Aisha again, holding something Megan recognised – a superhero comic book.

'Hi...' Megan began.

'Aisha! Come on! Let's go on the playing field!' Her friends were running up to her. Megan faltered.

'Hey, Megan. What is it?' Now the whole group was looking at her.

Come on, she told herself. This is just like that first time at Brownies. You can do this.

'I was just going to say that I've got that comic book too. I love superheroes.'

Aisha's eyes lit up. 'Oh yeah? I just LOVE Batman. I want to BE Batman! Who's your favourite?'

'Well,' said Megan, 'it used to be Violet from *The Incredibles*. You know, the one who could turn invisible? But now?' She grinned, thinking about how far she had come. 'Now, I'm not so sure.'

Win Brownie goodies!

Invent a new Brownie badge and you could win some awesome Brownie accessories!

If you've earned your Disability awareness or Environment badge, you'll know that Brownie badges can teach you a lot about yourself, your community and the wider world.

For a chance to win, all you need to do is come up with a badge inspired by something you care about. Saving badgers, getting rid of litter or staying safe online – it could be anything! Just send us your badge design and, in no more than 30 words, one thing a Brownie would need to do to earn it.

Post your competition entry (with your name and your unit's name) by 27 February 2015 to:

Brownie Annual 2015 Competition
Girlguiding
17-19 Buckingham Palace Road
London SW1W 0PT

TERMS & CONDITIONS
Entries must be received no later than 27 February 2015. The winning Brownie will be notified on or before 31 March 2015. Entries will be judged on creativity, effort and attention to detail. The judges' overall decision is final.

'We're completely full,' explained Willow, 'but this other unit doesn't have enough Brownies to stay open.'

'But Brownies is amazing!' exclaimed Megan. 'We should invite girls to a meeting so they can see for themselves!'

Together, they designed an invitation,

which the Leaders handed out at a local primary school. And a few weeks later they had a crowd of new faces to entertain!

Willow was smiling as the visitors left. 'Almost everyone said they wanted to join the other Brownie unit. Things are looking good!'

Now go to page 70 to find out how the story ends!

NEW!

A5 Lined Notepad
2190
£3.60

NEW DESIGN!

Sling Bag
42x29.5cm
8239
£3.20

NEW!

Doll
Height approx. 30cm
Not suitable for children under 36 months
2572
£9

NEW!

Brownie Flower Scented Soap
2189
£2.30

NEW DESIGN!

Roller Beaker
Height 10cm
8237
£3.75

Rubber Pin Badge
3cm
Not suitable for children under 36 months
7114
£1.25

'I've Done A Good Turn' Woven Badge
8528
80p

'Happiness Is' Woven Badge
8506
80p

NEW!

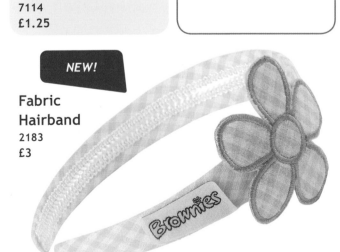

Fabric Hairband
2183
£3

NEW!

Cake Resin Bear
4.5cm
Not suitable for children under 36 months
2185
£1.75

NEW!

Boot Keyring
Height 6.5cm
2182
£2.10

0161 941 2237 to find your nearest volunteer shop or to order from the catalogue
www.girlguidingshop.co.uk to shop online

73

Animal superstars

How much do you know about amazing animals? Try this quiz to find out about some of the surprising things animals can do!

Match the facts to the pictures.

1 I can make the loudest sounds of any animal! (Even louder than Brownies!)

2 I can count up to four!

3 I can jump over 3 metres in the air! (That's higher than you standing on your friend's shoulders!)

4 Watch out – I can run faster than you!

5 I can smell my lunch from 18 miles away!

6 If I lose a leg, I can just grow a new one!

7 I can sleep for up to 22 hours a day! (Could you?)

8 I can swim at 65 miles per hour – over six times faster than the fastest human swimmer!

9 Scientists say I am cleverer than a three-year-old child!

10 I'm so strong, I can pull things that weigh 1,000 times as much as me! (That's like you pulling six double-decker buses full of people!)

Answers on page 77.

sailfish

dung beetle

bee

koala

pig

grizzly bear

hippo

red kangaroo

Badge link

octopus

blue whale

75

Puzzle and quiz answers

Pages 10-11 Puzzle time

Number crunchers
Beginner: 12
Intermediate: 57
Expert: 258

All mixed up
1. orange
2. grapefruit
3. raspberry
4. passion fruit
5. cherry
6. rhubarb
7. strawberry

Mind boggler
Here are some words you could have found: URNS, MINE, MIST, SEAT, SEAR, RATE, TENS, TARS, NEST, NEAT, NEAR, ERRS, EARS, EARN, ARTY, REST, TEST, TERN, TEAR, TURN, TYRE

Spot the difference

Pages 14-17 Detective Brownie and the Magna Carta mystery

Puzzle 1
THE BRITISH LIBRARY

Puzzle 2
MAGNA CARTA

Puzzle 3
Security guard

Puzzle 4

Puzzle 5
62462 22782

Pages 36-37 Hitting the headlines

1. England   3. Borneo   5. Australia
2. Canada   4. Mexico   6. Spain

Secret headline:
GIRL'S BRILLIANT BRAIN ASTOUNDS WORLD!

Pages 46–47 Tree teasers

Forest maze
1. Ash
2. Coast redwood
3. Maple syrup
4. Koala

Love your leaves
1. Holly
2. Oak
3. Maple
4. Willow
5. Beech
6. Rowan

Fruity fun
The missing fruit is pineapple!

M	T	N	D	B	N	O	M	E	L
C	A	O	E	A	H	S	G	P	I
A	P	R	I	C	O	T	O	E	M
H	P	A	P	H	I	M	L	A	E
N	L	N	K	E	A	B	N	R	I
O	E	G	O	R	F	G	E	S	C
S	C	E	M	R	O	F	R	M	E
M	A	R	I	Y	E	C	P	U	A
A	L	B	N	A	W	J	D	L	H
D	E	C	P	H	C	A	E	P	M

Pages 52–53 What's the password?

Crack the code
SHOUT

Pages 62–63 Number safari

Odd number out
a. 100
b. 101
c. 12
d. 6
e. 24
f. 8

The odd number out is 4!

Leap to safety
Start 3

Pages 54–55 Quiz-tastic!

Who am I?
1. Bart Simpson
2. Winnie-the-Pooh
3. Albert Einstein
4. Elizabeth I
5. Nelson Mandela

Picture it
1. Italy
2. Mo Farah
3. Sir Isaac Newton discovering gravity
4. The Mona Lisa (Leonardo da Vinci)
5. Ladybird

What's the link?
1. Bread
2. Bones
3. Deserts
4. Potatoes
5. National emblems (of England, Scotland, Ireland and Wales)

Literary legends

Katniss Everdeen	*The Hunger Games*
Andrea (Andy)	*The Suitcase Kid*
Belle	*Beauty and the Beast*
Dorothy	*The Wizard of Oz*
Hermione Granger	*Harry Potter and the Philosopher's Stone*

Pages 74–75 Animal superstars

1. Blue whale
2. Bee
3. Red kangaroo
4. Hippo
5. Grizzly bear
6. Octopus
7. Koala
8. Sailfish
9. Pig
10. Dung beetle

I love the fun activities we do.

We play games to keep us moving a bit.

We made pancakes at Brownies – tossing them was so much fun.

I love my Brownie uniform as it is so soft.

Brownies is an adventure!

We had a Brownie sleepover where we dressed up and did dancing.

We grew potato head cress men, then made egg and cress sandwiches.